Incredibly Easy
Cake Mix

Publications International, Ltd.
Favorite Brand Name Recipes at www.fbnr.com

Pictured on the front cover: Strawberry Shortcake *(page 18)*.
Pictured on the back cover: Elegant Chocolate Angel Torte *(page 90)*.

ISBN-13: 978-1-4127-2390-9
ISBN-10: 1-4127-2390-6

Library of Congress Control Number: 2006901734

Manufactured in China.

8 7 6 5 4 3 2 1

Microwave Cooking: Microwave ovens vary in wattage. Use the cooking times as guidelines and check for doneness before adding more time.

Preparation/Cooking Times: Preparation times are based on the approximate amount of time required to assemble the recipe before cooking, baking, chilling or serving. These times include preparation steps such as measuring, chopping and mixing. The fact that some preparations and cooking can be done simultaneously is taken into account.

Contents

Aunt Ruth's Favorite White Cake (p. 30)

Gingerbread Cake (p. 31)

Lemon Bars (p. 13)

Almond Cake (p. 23)

Classic Creations

Boston Cream Pie

½ (18¼-ounce) package light yellow cake mix
⅛ teaspoon baking soda
⅔ cup water
2 egg whites
1½ teaspoons vanilla, divided
1 package (4-serving size) sugar-free instant vanilla pudding and pie filling mix
1⅓ cups fat-free (skim) milk
Chocolate Glaze (recipe follows)

1. Preheat oven to 350°F. Spray 9-inch round cake pan with nonstick cooking spray. Lightly coat with flour. Set aside.

2. Combine cake mix and baking soda in large bowl; mix well. Add water, egg whites and 1 teaspoon vanilla. Beat with electric mixer at low speed 30 seconds. Increase speed to medium; beat 2 minutes.

3. Pour batter into prepared pan. Bake 30 minutes or until cake pulls away from side of pan and springs back when touched lightly in center. Remove from oven. Cool 10 minutes on wire rack. Invert onto serving plate; cool completely.

4. Combine pudding mix, milk and remaining ½ teaspoon vanilla in medium bowl. Beat at low speed with electric mixer 2 minutes; set aside.

5. Prepare Chocolate Glaze.

6. Cut cake in half horizontally; carefully remove top half of cake. Spread bottom half with pudding mixture. Replace top half; spoon Chocolate Glaze over top. Allow to stand until glaze hardens. Cut into wedges.

Makes 8 servings

Chocolate Glaze: Sift together ⅔ cup powdered sugar and 1 tablespoon unsweetened cocoa powder in medium bowl. Add 1 tablespoon water and ½ teaspoon vanilla; mix well. Add more water, 1 teaspoon at a time, until of desired spreading consistency.

Chocolate Bundt Cake with White Chocolate Glaze

Prep Time: 10 minutes • Bake Time: 40 minutes

Cake
- **1 package (18¼ ounces) chocolate cake mix**
- **3 whole eggs** *or* **¾ cup cholesterol-free egg substitute**
- **3 jars (2½ ounces each) puréed baby food prunes**
- **¾ cup warm water**
- **2 to 3 teaspoons instant coffee granules**
- **2 tablespoons canola oil**

Glaze
- **½ cup white chocolate chips**
- **1 tablespoon milk**

1. Preheat oven to 350°F. Lightly grease and flour bundt pan; set aside.

2. Combine all cake ingredients in large bowl. Beat with electric mixer at high speed 2 minutes. Pour into prepared pan. Bake 40 minutes or until toothpick inserted in center comes out clean; cool 10 minutes. Invert cake onto serving plate; cool completely.

3. To prepare glaze, combine white chocolate chips and milk in small microwavable bowl. Microwave on MEDIUM (50%) 50 seconds; stir. Microwave on MEDIUM at additional 30-second intervals until chips are completely melted; stir well after each 30-second interval.

4. Pour warm glaze over cooled cake. Let stand about 30 minutes. Garnish as desired; serve. *Makes 16 servings*

Tip: To grease and flour cake pans, use a paper towel, waxed paper or your fingers to apply a thin, even layer of shortening. Sprinkle flour into the greased pan; shake or tilt the pan to coat evenly with flour, then tap lightly to remove any excess.

Black Forest Torte

1 package DUNCAN HINES® Moist Deluxe® Dark Chocolate Fudge Cake Mix
2½ cups whipping cream, chilled
2½ tablespoons confectioners' sugar
1 (21-ounce) can cherry pie filling

1. Preheat oven to 350°F. Grease and flour two 9-inch round cake pans.

2. Prepare, bake and cool cake as directed on package.

3. Beat whipping cream in large bowl until soft peaks form. Add sugar gradually. Beat until stiff peaks form.

4. To assemble, place one cake layer on serving plate. Spread two-thirds cherry pie filling on cake to within ½ inch of edge. Spread 1½ cups whipped cream mixture over cherry pie filling. Top with second cake layer. Frost sides and top with remaining whipped cream mixture. Spread remaining cherry pie filling on top to within 1 inch of edge. Refrigerate until ready to serve.   *Makes 12 to 16 servings*

Tip: Chill the cherry pie filling for easy spreading on cake. Also, garnish the cake with grated semisweet chocolate or white chocolate curls.

Easy Turtle Squares

1 package (18¼ ounces) chocolate cake mix
½ cup (1 stick) butter, melted
¼ cup milk
1 cup (6 ounces) semisweet chocolate chips
1 cup chopped pecans
1 jar (12 ounces) caramel ice cream topping

1. Preheat oven to 350°F. Spray 13×9-inch baking pan with nonstick cooking spray.

2. Combine cake mix, butter and milk in large bowl. Press half of mixture into prepared pan.

3. Bake 7 to 8 minutes or until crust begins to form; remove from oven. Sprinkle chocolate chips and half of pecans over partially baked crust. Drizzle caramel topping over chips and pecans. Drop spoonfuls of remaining cake batter over caramel; sprinkle with remaining pecans.

4. Bake 18 to 20 minutes or until top springs back when lightly touched. (Caramel center will be soft.) Cool completely on wire rack. Cut into squares.   *Makes 24 squares*

Lemon Bars

1 package DUNCAN HINES® Moist Deluxe® Lemon Supreme Cake Mix
3 eggs, divided
⅓ cup butter-flavor shortening
½ cup granulated sugar
¼ cup lemon juice
2 teaspoons grated lemon peel
½ teaspoon baking powder
¼ teaspoon salt
Confectioners' sugar

1. Preheat oven to 350°F.

2. Combine cake mix, 1 egg and shortening in large mixing bowl. Beat at low speed with electric mixer until crumbs form. Reserve 1 cup. Pat remaining mixture lightly into *ungreased* 13×9-inch pan. Bake at 350°F for 15 minutes or until lightly browned.

3. Combine remaining 2 eggs, granulated sugar, lemon juice, lemon peel, baking powder and salt in medium mixing bowl. Beat at medium speed with electric mixer until light and foamy. Pour over hot crust. Sprinkle with reserved crumb mixture.

4. Bake at 350°F for 15 minutes or until lightly browned. Sprinkle with confectioners' sugar. Cool in pan. Cut into bars.   *Makes 30 to 32 bars*

Tip: These bars are also delicious using Duncan Hines® Moist Deluxe® Classic Yellow Cake Mix.

Carrot Layer Cake

Cake

 1 package DUNCAN HINES® Moist Deluxe® Classic Yellow Cake Mix

 4 eggs

 ½ cup vegetable oil

 3 cups grated carrots

 1 cup finely chopped nuts

 2 teaspoons ground cinnamon

Cream Cheese Frosting

 1 package (8 ounces) cream cheese, softened

 ¼ cup butter or margarine, softened

 2 teaspoons vanilla extract

 4 cups confectioners' sugar

 Whole pecans

1. Preheat oven to 350°F. Grease and flour two 8- or 9-inch round baking pans.

2. For cake, combine cake mix, eggs, oil, carrots, nuts and cinnamon in large bowl. Beat at low speed with electric mixer until moistened. Beat at medium speed for 2 minutes. Pour into prepared pans. Bake at 350°F for 35 to 40 minutes or until toothpick inserted into centers comes out clean. Cool.

3. For cream cheese frosting, place cream cheese, butter and vanilla extract in large bowl. Beat at low speed until smooth and creamy. Add confectioners' sugar gradually, beating until smooth. Add more sugar to thicken, or milk or water to thin frosting, as needed. Fill and frost cooled cake. Garnish with whole pecans. *Makes 12 to 16 servings*

Banana Fudge Layer Cake

1 package DUNCAN HINES® Moist Deluxe® Yellow Cake Mix
1⅓ cups water
3 eggs
⅓ cup vegetable oil
1 cup mashed ripe bananas (about 3 medium)
1 container DUNCAN HINES® Chocolate Frosting

1. Preheat oven to 350°F. Grease and flour two 9-inch round cake pans.

2. Combine cake mix, water, eggs and oil in large bowl. Beat at low speed with electric mixer until moistened. Beat at medium speed 2 minutes. Stir in bananas.

3. Pour into prepared pans. Bake at 350°F for 28 to 31 minutes or until toothpick inserted in center comes out clean. Cool in pans 15 minutes. Remove from pans; cool completely.

4. Fill and frost cake with frosting. Garnish as desired.

Makes 12 to 16 servings

Strawberry Shortcake

4 cups strawberries, hulled and sliced
2 tablespoons granulated sugar
**1 package (18¼ ounces) yellow cake mix, plus ingredients
  to prepare mix**
**1 container (12 ounces) frozen whipped topping, thawed
  Mint sprig (optional)**

1. Preheat oven to 350°F. Grease and flour two 8-inch round baking pans.

2. Combine strawberries and sugar. Refrigerate until ready to use.

3. Prepare and bake cake mix according to package directions.

4. Place one cake layer on serving plate. Spread ⅓ of whipped topping over cake. Top with ¾ of strawberries and another ⅓ of whipped topping. Place second cake layer over whipped topping. Dollop remaining ⅓ whipped topping in center of cake and garnish with remaining strawberries and mint sprig, if desired. (Slices may also be garnished individually.)   *Makes 16 servings*

Creamy Coconut Cake with Almond Filling

1 package (18¼ ounces) white cake mix
1 cup sour cream
3 eggs
½ cup vegetable oil
1 teaspoon vanilla
1 teaspoon coconut extract
1 can (12½ ounces) almond filling
2 containers (16 ounces each) creamy coconut frosting
½ cup sliced almonds

1. Preheat oven to 350°F. Grease and flour two 9-inch round baking pans.

2. Combine cake mix, sour cream, eggs, oil, vanilla and coconut extract in large bowl. Beat with electric mixer at low speed 3 minutes or until well blended. Divide evenly between prepared pans. Bake 30 to 35 minutes or until toothpicks inserted into centers come out clean. Cool completely in pans on wire racks.

3. Remove cakes from pans. Slice each cake horizontally in half to make 4 layers. Place one cake layer on serving plate; spread with half of almond filling. Top with second cake layer; spread with ½ cup coconut frosting. Top with third cake layer; spread with remaining almond filling. Top with fourth cake layer; spread remaining coconut frosting over top and side of cake. Sprinkle with almonds. *Makes 8 to 12 servings*

Butterscotch Bundt Cake

1 package (18¼ ounces) yellow cake mix *without* pudding in the mix
1 package (4-serving size) butterscotch-flavor instant pudding and pie filling mix
1 cup water
3 eggs
2 teaspoons ground cinnamon
½ cup chopped pecans
Powdered sugar (optional)

Preheat oven to 325°F. Spray 12-cup bundt pan with nonstick cooking spray. Combine all ingredients except pecans and powdered sugar in large bowl. Beat with electric mixer at medium-high speed 2 minutes or until blended. Stir in pecans. Pour into prepared pan. Bake 40 to 50 minutes or until cake springs back when lightly touched. Cool in pan on wire rack 10 minutes. Invert cake onto serving plate and cool completely. Sprinkle with powdered sugar, if desired.   *Makes 12 to 16 servings*

Pistachio Walnut Bundt Cake: Substitute white cake mix for yellow cake mix, pistachio-flavored pudding mix for butterscotch-flavored pudding mix and walnuts for pecans. Prepare as directed above.

Almond
Cake

1 can (8 ounces) almond paste
3 eggs
1 package (18¼ ounces) white cake mix
1¼ cups water
⅓ cup vegetable oil
1 container (12 ounces) whipped vanilla frosting, divided
1 tablespoon seedless raspberry preserves
Candy-coated almonds for garnish

1. Preheat oven to 350°F. Grease two 9-inch round cake pans. Line bottom of pans with parchment paper; spray parchment with nonstick cooking spray.

2. Place almond paste and eggs in large mixing bowl; stir until smooth and no lumps remain.

3. Add cake mix, water and oil to almond paste mixture. Beat 1 minute on low speed of electric mixer. Beat 2 minutes on medium-low or until well blended.

4. Divide batter evenly between cake pans. Bake 35 minutes or until toothpick inserted into centers comes out clean. Cool completely in pans on wire racks; remove cakes from pans.

5. For filling, place ¼ cup frosting into small bowl; stir in preserves. Place one layer on serving plate. Spread filling onto top of layer to within ¼ inch of edge. Top with remaining layer. Frost sides and top of cake with remaining white frosting. Decorate with almonds.   *Makes 12 servings*

German Chocolate Cake

Prep Time: 15 minutes • Bake Time: 40 to 45 minutes

1 (18.25-ounce) package chocolate cake mix
1 cup water
3 eggs
½ cup vegetable oil
1 (14-ounce) can EAGLE BRAND® Sweetened Condensed Milk (NOT evaporated milk), divided
3 tablespoons butter or margarine
1 egg yolk
⅓ cup chopped pecans
⅓ cup flaked coconut
1 teaspoon vanilla extract

1. Preheat oven to 350°F. Grease and flour 13×9-inch baking pan. In large bowl, combine cake mix, water, 3 eggs, oil and ⅓ cup EAGLE BRAND®. Beat at low speed of electric mixer until moistened; beat at high speed 2 minutes.

2. Pour into prepared pan. Bake 40 to 45 minutes or until wooden pick inserted near center comes out clean.

3. In small saucepan over medium heat, combine remaining EAGLE BRAND®, butter and egg yolk. Cook and stir until thickened, about 6 minutes. Add pecans, coconut and vanilla; spread over warm cake. Store leftovers covered in refrigerator. *Makes 10 to 12 servings*

Chocolate-Raspberry Layer Cake

2 packages (18¼ ounces each) chocolate cake mix, plus ingredients to prepare mixes
1 jar (10 ounces) seedless red raspberry fruit spread
1 package (12 ounces) white chocolate chips, divided
1 container (16 ounces) chocolate frosting
½ pint fresh raspberries
1 to 2 cups toasted sliced almonds

1. Preheat oven to 350°F. Grease and flour four 9-inch round cake pans. Prepare cake mixes according to package directions. Divide batter evenly between prepared pans. Bake as directed on package. Cool completely.

2. Place one cake layer on serving plate. Spread with ⅓ of fruit spread. Sprinkle with ½ cup white chocolate chips. Repeat with second and third cake layers, fruit spread and white chocolate chips.

3. Place fourth cake layer on top. Frost top and side of cake with chocolate frosting. Decorate top of cake in alternating concentric circles of raspberries and remaining ½ cup white chocolate chips. Press almonds into frosting on side of cake. *Makes 8 to 10 servings*

Pumpkin Bread

1 package (about 18 ounces) yellow cake mix
1 can (16 ounces) solid pack pumpkin
4 eggs
⅓ cup GRANDMA'S® Molasses
1 teaspoon cinnamon
1 teaspoon nutmeg
⅓ cup nuts, chopped (optional)
⅓ cup raisins (optional)

Preheat oven to 350°F. Grease two 9×5-inch loaf pans.

Combine all ingredients in large bowl and mix well. Beat at medium speed 2 minutes. Pour into prepared pans. Bake 60 minutes or until toothpick inserted into center comes out clean.   *Makes 2 loaves*

Tip: Serve with cream cheese or preserves, or top with cream cheese frosting or ice cream.

Aunt Ruth's Favorite White Cake

1 package (18¼ ounces) white cake mix
1¼ cups water
3 eggs
2 tablespoons vegetable oil
1 teaspoon vanilla
½ teaspoon almond extract
Creamy White Frosting (recipe follows)

1. Preheat oven to 350°F. Grease and flour two 8- or 9-inch round cake pans.

2. Combine cake mix, water, eggs and oil in large bowl. Beat at medium speed of electric mixer until well blended. Add vanilla and almond extract; mix until well blended. Divide batter evenly between prepared pans.

3. Bake 30 to 35 minutes or until toothpicks inserted into centers come out clean. Cool in pans on wire racks 10 minutes. Remove cakes from pans to racks; cool completely.

4. Prepare Creamy White Frosting. Fill and frost cake with frosting.

Makes one 2-layer cake

Creamy White Frosting

1 cup milk
3 tablespoons all-purpose flour
1 cup (2 sticks) butter, softened
1 cup powdered sugar
1 teaspoon vanilla

1. Combine milk and flour in medium saucepan; cook and stir over low heat until thickened. Cool.

2. Beat butter in large bowl until creamy. Add powdered sugar; beat until fluffy. Blend in vanilla. Add milk mixture; beat until thick and smooth.

Makes about ½ cup frosting

Gingerbread Cake

1 package (18¼ ounces) yellow cake mix, plus ingredients to prepare mix
½ cup molasses
2 teaspoons ground cinnamon
1½ teaspoons ground ginger
¼ teaspoon ground nutmeg
Powdered sugar (optional)

1. Preheat oven to 350°F. Grease and flour 9×9-inch baking pan.

2. Prepare cake mix according to package directions. Add molasses, cinnamon, ginger and nutmeg. Beat with electric mixer at medium speed 2 minutes or until well blended. Pour into prepared pan.

3. Bake 25 to 30 minutes or until toothpick inserted into center comes out clean. Cool completely in pan on wire rack. Sprinkle with powdered sugar, if desired. *Makes 10 to 12 servings*

**Blueberry Cream Cheese
Pound Cake (p. 39)**

**Apple-Walnut Glazed
Spice Baby Cakes (p. 47)**

Lemon-Orange
Party Cake (p.52)

Double Berry Layer Cake (p. 57)

Fruitful Occasions

Pineapple Almond Coffeecake

Prep Time: 14 minutes

1 can (8 ounces) crushed pineapple in juice, undrained
1 teaspoon cornstarch
1 tablespoon grated orange peel
1 package (9 ounces) golden yellow cake mix
⅓ cup water
1 large egg
¼ cup sliced almonds
1 tablespoon powdered sugar (optional)

1. Preheat oven to 350°F.

2. Combine pineapple with juice and cornstarch in small saucepan; stir until cornstarch is completely dissolved. Bring to a boil over medium-high heat; continue to boil 1 minute, stirring frequently. Remove from heat; add orange peel. Set aside to cool slightly.

3. Combine cake mix, water and egg in medium bowl. Beat according to package directions.

4. Coat 9-inch springform pan with nonstick cooking spray. Pour half of batter into prepared pan. Spoon pineapple mixture evenly over batter. Do not stir into batter. Gently spoon remaining batter evenly over all. Top with almonds. Bake 30 minutes or until cake is golden and springs back when lightly pressed with fingertips. Remove to wire rack; cool completely.

5. Sprinkle powdered sugar over top, if desired. Cut into 10 wedges to serve.   *Makes 10 servings*

Note: This cake will be puffy when it is removed from the oven, but will settle upon cooling.

Topsy-Turvy
Banana Crunch Cake

⅓ **cup uncooked old-fashioned oats**
3 **tablespoons packed brown sugar**
1 **tablespoon all-purpose flour**
¼ **teaspoon ground cinnamon**
2 **tablespoons butter**
2 **tablespoons coarsely chopped pecans**
1 **package (9 ounces) yellow cake mix** *without* **pudding in
  the mix**
½ **cup sour cream**
½ **cup mashed banana (about 1 medium)**
1 **slightly beaten egg**

1. Preheat oven to 350°F. Lightly grease 8-inch square baking pan.

2. Combine oats, brown sugar, flour and cinnamon in small bowl. Cut in butter with pastry blender or 2 knives until crumbly. Stir in pecans.

3. Combine cake mix, sour cream, banana and egg in medium bowl. Beat with electric mixer at low speed about 1 minute or until blended. Increase speed to medium; beat 1 to 2 minutes or until smooth. Spoon half of batter into prepared pan; sprinkle with half of oat topping. Top with remaining battter and topping.

4. Bake 25 to 30 minutes or until toothpick inserted into center comes out clean. Cool completely on wire rack.   *Makes 9 servings*

Apricot Crumb Squares

1 package (18¼ ounces) yellow cake mix
1 teaspoon ground cinnamon
½ teaspoon ground nutmeg
¼ cup plus 2 tablespoons cold margarine, cut into pieces
¾ cup uncooked multigrain oatmeal cereal or
    old-fashioned oats
1 whole egg
2 egg whites
1 tablespoon water
1 jar (10 ounces) apricot fruit spread
2 tablespoons packed light brown sugar

1. Preheat oven to 350°F. Combine cake mix, cinnamon and nutmeg in medium bowl. Cut in margarine with pastry blender or 2 knives until coarse crumbs form. Stir in cereal. Reserve 1 cup crumb mixture. Add egg, egg whites and water to remaining crumb mixture; stir until well blended.

2. Spread evenly in ungreased 13×9-inch baking pan; top with fruit spread. Sprinkle reserved crumb mixture over fruit spread; sprinkle with brown sugar.

3. Bake 35 to 40 minutes or until top is golden brown. Cool in pan on wire rack; cut into 15 squares. *Makes 15 servings*

Blueberry Cream Cheese Pound Cake

1 package (16 ounces) pound cake mix, divided
1½ cups fresh blueberries
5 ounces cream cheese, softened
2 eggs
¾ cup milk
Powdered sugar (optional)

1. Preheat oven to 350°F. Grease 9×5×2-inch loaf pan.

2. Place ¼ cup cake mix in medium bowl; add blueberries and toss until well coated.

3. Beat cream cheese in large bowl 1 minute on medium speed of electric mixer until light and fluffy. Add eggs, one at a time, beating well after each addition.

4. Add remaining cake mix alternately with milk, beginning and ending with cake mix, beating well after each addition. Beat 1 minute on medium speed or until light and fluffy.

5. Fold blueberry mixture into batter. Pour mixture into prepared pan. Bake 55 to 60 minutes or until toothpick inserted into center comes out clean.

6. Cool in pan on wire rack 10 minutes. Remove cake to wire rack; cool completely. Lightly sprinkle top with powdered sugar, if desired.

Makes 1 (9-inch) pound cake

Berry Cobbler Cake

2 cups (1 pint) fresh or frozen berries (blueberries, blackberries, and/or raspberries)
1 package (9 ounces) yellow cake mix
1 teaspoon ground cinnamon
1 egg
1 cup water, divided
¼ cup sugar
1 tablespoon cornstarch
Ice cream (optional)

1. Preheat oven to 375°F.

2. Place berries in 9-inch square baking pan; set aside.

3. Combine cake mix and cinnamon in large bowl. Add egg and ¼ cup water; stir until well blended. Spoon over berries.

4. Combine sugar and cornstarch in small bowl. Stir in remaining ¾ cup water until sugar mixture dissolves; pour over cake batter.

5. Bake 40 to 45 minutes or until lightly browned. Serve warm or at room temperature with ice cream, if desired.   *Makes 6 servings*

Mandarin Orange Tea Cake

1 package (16 ounces) pound cake mix
½ cup plus 2 tablespoons orange juice, divided
2 eggs
¼ cup milk
1 can (15 ounces) mandarin orange segments in light syrup, drained
¾ cup powdered sugar
Grated peel of 1 orange

1. Preheat oven to 350°F. Grease 9-inch bundt pan.

2. Beat cake mix, ½ cup orange juice, eggs and milk in large bowl with electric mixer at medium speed 2 minutes or until light and fluffy. Fold in orange segments. Pour batter into prepared pan.

3. Bake 45 minutes or until golden brown and toothpick inserted near center comes out clean. Cool in pan 15 minutes on wire rack. Invert cake onto wire rack; cool completely.

4. Combine sugar, orange peel and remaining 2 tablespoons orange juice in small bowl; stir until smooth. Drizzle glaze over cake. Allow glaze to set about 5 minutes before serving.   *Makes 16 servings*

Luscious Lime
Angel Food Cake Rolls

1 package (16 ounces) angel food cake mix
2 drops green food coloring (optional)
2 containers (8 ounces each) lime-flavored yogurt
Lime slices (optional)

1. Preheat oven to 350°F. Line two 17×11¼×1-inch jelly-roll pans with parchment or waxed paper; set aside.

2. Prepare cake mix according to package directions. Divide batter evenly between prepared pans. Draw knife through batter to remove large air bubbles. Bake 12 minutes or until cakes are lightly browned and toothpick inserted into centers comes out clean.

3. Invert each cake onto separate clean towel. Starting at short end, roll up warm cakes, jelly-roll fashion, with towel inside. Cool cakes completely.

4. Place 1 to 2 drops green food coloring in each container of yogurt, if desired; stir well. Unroll cakes; remove towels. Spread each cake with 1 container yogurt, leaving 1-inch border. Roll up cakes; place seam side down. Slice each cake roll into 8 pieces. Garnish with lime slices, if desired. Serve immediately or refrigerate. *Makes 16 servings*

Cran-Raspberry Cake

1 package (16 ounces) light pound cake mix, plus ingredients to prepare mix
1½ teaspoons WATKINS® Butter Extract
1½ teaspoons WATKINS® Vanilla
1 pie filling recipe WATKINS® Vanilla Dessert Mix, plus ingredients to prepare filling
1 cup cranberry or cran-raspberry juice cocktail
2 cups fresh raspberries *or* 2 packages (10 to 12 ounces each) frozen raspberries, thawed
2 tablespoons sugar
8 ounces reduced-fat whipped topping
Additional fresh raspberries for garnish

Prepare pound cake mix according to package directions, stirring extracts into batter. Bake according to package directions and cool completely. Prepare dessert mix according to package directions using recipe for pie filling; cool completely.

Cut pound cake into ½- to ¾-inch slices; place one slice on each dessert plate. Drizzle each slice with 1 tablespoon juice, top with raspberries and sprinkle with ½ teaspoon sugar. Gently stir 1 cup whipped topping into pie filling and spoon mixture over raspberries. Top with remaining whipped topping. Refrigerate until ready to serve. Garnish with additional berries just before serving.   *Makes 12 servings*

Variation: For red, white and blue cake, add blueberries to the raspberries in the recipe.

Apple-Walnut Glazed Spice Baby Cakes

All-purpose flour for dusting
1 package (18¼ ounces) spice cake mix
1⅓ cups plus 3 tablespoons water, divided
3 eggs
⅓ cup vegetable oil
½ teaspoon vanilla butter and nut flavoring*
¾ cup chopped walnuts
12 ounces Granny Smith apples, peeled and cut into
½-inch cubes (about 2 apples)
¼ teaspoon ground cinnamon
1 jar (12 ounces) caramel ice cream topping

*Vanilla butter and nut flavoring is available in the baking section of most large supermarkets.

1. Preheat oven to 350°F. Lightly grease and flour 12 (1-cup) mini bundt pans.

2. Beat cake mix, 1⅓ cups water, eggs, oil and flavoring in large bowl with electric mixer at low speed 30 seconds. Beat 2 minutes at medium speed.

3. Spoon batter evenly into prepared pans. Bake 25 minutes or until toothpick inserted near centers of cakes comes out almost clean. Cool in pans on wire racks 15 minutes. Carefully invert cakes from pans to wire racks; cool completely.

4. Meanwhile, place 12-inch skillet over medium high heat until hot. Add walnuts; cook 3 minutes or until walnuts are lightly browned, stirring frequently. Remove nuts to small bowl. In same skillet, combine apples, remaining 3 tablespoons water and cinnamon; cook and stir over medium-high heat 3 minutes or until apples are crisp-tender. Remove from heat; stir in walnuts and caramel topping. Spoon glaze over each cake. *Makes 12 cakes*

Lemon-Up
Cakes

1 package (18¼ ounces) butter recipe cake mix with pudding in the mix, plus ingredients to prepare mix
½ cup fresh lemon juice, divided (2 large lemons)
Grated peel of 2 lemons, divided
½ cup (1 stick) butter, at room temperature
3½ cups powdered sugar
Yellow food coloring
1 package (9½ ounces) lemon-shaped hard candies, coarsely crushed

1. Preheat oven to 350°F. Line 24 standard (2½-inch) muffin pan cups with paper liners.

2. Prepare cake mix according to package directions using ¼ cup less water than directions call for. Stir in ¼ cup lemon juice and half of grated lemon peel. Fill muffin cups ⅔ full.

3. Bake 23 minutes or until light golden brown and toothpick inserted into centers comes out clean. Cool cupcakes in pans on wire racks 5 minutes; remove from pans and cool completely on wire racks.

4. For frosting, beat butter in large bowl with electric mixer at medium speed until creamy. Gradually add powdered sugar to form stiff mixture. Add remaining ¼ cup lemon juice, lemon peel and several drops food coloring. Beat at high speed until frosting is light and fluffy.

5. Generously frost cupcakes. Sprinkle crushed candies over frosting.

Makes 24 cupcakes

Crunchy Peach Snack Cake

1 package (9 ounces) yellow cake mix *without* pudding in the mix

1 container (6 ounces) peach-flavor yogurt

1 egg

¼ cup peach all-fruit spread

¾ cup square whole grain oat cereal with cinnamon, slightly crushed

Whipped cream (optional)

1. Place rack in center of oven; preheat oven to 350°F. Lightly grease 8-inch square baking pan.

2. Combine cake mix, yogurt and egg in medium bowl. Beat with electric mixer at low speed about 1 minute or until blended. Increase speed to medium; beat 1 to 2 minutes or until smooth.

3. Spread batter in prepared pan. Drop fruit spread by ½ teaspoonfuls over cake batter. Sprinkle with crushed cereal.

4. Bake about 25 minutes or until toothpick inserted into center of cake comes out clean. Cool on wire rack. Serve with whipped cream, if desired.

Makes 9 servings

Lemon-Orange Party Cake

1 package (18¼ ounces) yellow cake mix with pudding in the mix
1¼ cups plus 5 tablespoons orange juice, divided
3 eggs
⅓ cup vegetable oil
2 tablespoons grated orange peel
5½ cups sifted powdered sugar, divided
⅓ cup lemon juice
⅓ cup butter, softened
Multi-colored sprinkles
20 jellied orange or lemon slices

1. Preheat oven to 350°F. Lightly grease 13×9-inch baking pan.

2. Beat cake mix, 1¼ cups orange juice, eggs, oil and orange peel in large bowl with electric mixer at low speed about 1 minute or until blended. Increase speed to medium; beat 1 to 2 minutes or until smooth. Spread in prepared pan.

3. Bake 33 to 38 minutes or until toothpick inserted into center comes out clean. Meanwhile, combine 1 cup powdered sugar and lemon juice in small bowl; stir until smooth.

4. Pierce top of warm cake generously with large fork or wooden skewer (about ½-inch intervals). Slowly drizzle lemon glaze over warm cake. Cool completely.

5. Beat remaining 4½ cups powdered sugar and butter in large bowl with electric mixer on low speed until combined. Beat in enough of remaining orange juice to reach spreading consistency. Gently spread frosting over cooled cake. Decorate top of cake with sprinkles and candied fruit slices.

Makes 20 servings

Raspberry Buckle
Cupcakes

½ package (18-ounce) refrigerated sugar cookie dough*
½ cup all-purpose flour
¼ cup firmly packed light brown sugar
1 teaspoon vanilla
½ cup slivered almonds
**1 package (18¼ ounces) lemon cake mix, plus ingredients
  to prepare mix**
1 can (12 ounces) raspberry pie filling

Save remaining ½ package of dough for another use.

1. Preheat oven to 350°F. Line 24 standard (2½-inch) muffin pan cups with paper or foil baking cups.

2. For topping, combine cookie dough, flour, brown sugar and vanilla in large bowl; beat until well blended. Stir in almonds; set aside.

3. Prepare cake mix according to package directions. Divide batter evenly among prepared muffin pan cups; place 1 tablespoon pie filling on batter in each muffin cup. Bake 10 minutes.

4. Sprinkle cookie topping evenly over partially baked cupcakes. Bake 15 minutes or until topping is browned and cupcakes are set.

Makes 2 dozen cupcakes

Cherry Pudding
Cake

**1 (18¼-ounce) package yellow cake mix, plus ingredients
  to prepare mix**
1 (8-ounce) package cream cheese, softened
2 cups milk, divided
1 (3-ounce) package instant vanilla pudding
1 (21-ounce) can cherry pie filling

Prepare cake mix according to package directions. Pour batter into greased 13×9×2-inch baking pan. Bake as directed on package. Let cake cool in pan.

Combine cream cheese and ½ cup milk in small bowl. Beat with electric mixer on medium speed 3 to 4 minutes or until smooth. Add pudding mix and remaining 1½ cups milk; mix well. Let mixture stand until thick. Pour cream cheese mixture over cool cake. Top with cherry pie filling. Refrigerate, covered, until ready to serve.   *Makes about 15 servings*

Favorite recipe from **Cherry Marketing Institute**

Double Berry Layer Cake

1 package DUNCAN HINES® Moist Deluxe® Strawberry Supreme Cake Mix
⅔ cup strawberry jam
2½ cups fresh blueberries, rinsed, drained
1 container (8 ounces) frozen whipped topping, thawed Fresh strawberry slices for garnish

1. Preheat oven to 350°F. Grease and flour two 9-inch round cake pans.

2. Prepare, bake and cool cake following package directions for basic recipe.

3. Place one cake layer on serving plate. Spread with ⅓ cup strawberry jam. Arrange 1 cup blueberries on jam. Spread half the whipped topping to within ½ inch of cake edge. Place second cake layer on top. Repeat with remaining ⅓ cup strawberry jam, 1 cup blueberries and remaining whipped topping. Garnish with strawberry slices and remaining ½ cup blueberries. Refrigerate until ready to serve.   *Makes 12 servings*

Tip: For best results, cut cake with serrated knife; clean knife after each slice.

Sweet Mysteries (p. 66)

Peanut Butter
Cheesecake Bars (p. 77)

Pastel Mint Swirls (p. 84)

Sunshine Sandwiches (p. 85)

Cookies & Bars

Cinnamon Cereal Crispies

½ **cup granulated sugar**
2 **teaspoons ground cinnamon, divided**
1 **package (18¼ ounces) white or yellow cake mix with pudding in the mix**
½ **cup water**
⅓ **cup vegetable oil**
1 **egg**
2 **cups crisp rice cereal**
1 **cup cornflakes**
1 **cup raisins**
1 **cup chopped nuts (optional)**

1. Preheat oven to 350°F. Lightly spray cookie sheets with nonstick cooking spray. Combine sugar and 1 teaspoon cinnamon in small bowl; set aside.

2. Beat cake mix, water, oil, egg and remaining 1 teaspoon cinnamon in large bowl with electric mixer at medium speed 1 minute. Gently stir in rice cereal, cornflakes, raisins and nuts, if desired, until well blended.

3. Drop batter by rounded tablespoonfuls 2 inches apart onto prepared cookie sheets. Sprinkle lightly with reserved cinnamon-sugar mixture.

4. Bake about 15 minutes or until lightly browned. Sprinkle cookies with additional cinnamon-sugar mixture after baking; transfer to wire racks to cool completely. *Makes about 5 dozen cookies*

Orange Coconut Cream Bars

1 (18¼-ounce) package yellow cake mix
1 cup quick-cooking or old-fashioned oats, uncooked
¾ cup chopped nuts
½ cup butter or margarine, melted
1 large egg
1 (14-ounce) can sweetened condensed milk
2 teaspoons grated orange zest
1 cup shredded coconut
1 cup "M&M's"® Semi-Sweet Chocolate Mini Baking Bits

Preheat oven to 375°F. Lightly grease 13×9×2-inch baking pan; set aside. In large bowl combine cake mix, oats, nuts, butter and egg until ingredients are thoroughly moistened and mixture resembles coarse crumbs. Reserve 1 cup mixture. Firmly press remaining mixture onto bottom of prepared pan; bake 10 minutes. In separate bowl combine condensed milk and orange zest; spread over baked base. Combine reserved crumb mixture, coconut and "M&M's"® Semi-Sweet Chocolate Mini Baking Bits; sprinkle evenly over condensed milk mixture and press in lightly. Continue baking 20 to 25 minutes or until golden brown. Cool completely. Cut into bars. Store in tightly covered container.

Makes 26 bars

Festive Fudge Blossoms

Prep and Bake Time: 30 minutes

¼ cup (½ stick) butter, softened
1 package (18¼ ounces) chocolate fudge cake mix
1 egg, lightly beaten
2 tablespoons water
¾ to 1 cup finely chopped walnuts
48 chocolate star candies

1. Preheat oven to 350°F. Cut butter into cake mix in large bowl until mixture resembles coarse crumbs. Stir in egg and water until well blended.

2. Shape dough into ½-inch balls; roll in walnuts, pressing nuts gently into dough. Place about 2 inches apart on ungreased baking sheets.

3. Bake cookies 12 minutes or until puffed and nearly set. Place chocolate star in center of each cookie; bake 1 minute. Cool 2 minutes on baking sheets. Remove cookies from baking sheets to wire racks to cool completely. *Makes 4 dozen cookies*

Sweet Mysteries

1 package (18¼ ounces) yellow cake mix with pudding in the mix
½ cup (1 stick) unsalted butter, softened
1 egg yolk
1 cup ground pecans
36 milk chocolate candy kisses
Powdered sugar

1. Preheat oven to 300°F.

2. Beat half of cake mix and butter in large bowl with electric mixer at high speed until light. Add egg yolk and remaining cake mix; beat at medium speed just until dough forms. Add pecans; beat just until blended.

3. Shape rounded tablespoon of dough around each candy, making sure candy is completely covered. Place cookies 1 inch apart on ungreased cookie sheets.

4. Bake 20 to 25 minutes or until firm and just beginning to turn golden. Let cookies stand on cookie sheets 10 minutes. Transfer to wire racks set over waxed paper; dust with powdered sugar.   *Makes 3 dozen cookies*

Chocolate Macaroon Squares

1 package (18.25 ounce) chocolate cake mix
⅓ cup butter or margarine, softened
1 large egg, lightly beaten
1 can (14 ounces) NESTLÉ® CARNATION® Sweetened Condensed Milk
1 large egg
1 teaspoon vanilla extract
1⅓ cups flaked sweetened coconut, *divided*
1 cup chopped pecans
1 cup (6 ounces) NESTLÉ® TOLL HOUSE® Semi-Sweet Chocolate Morsels

PREHEAT oven to 350°F.

COMBINE cake mix, butter and egg in large bowl; mix with fork until crumbly. Press onto bottom of ungreased 13×9-inch baking pan. Combine sweetened condensed milk, egg and vanilla extract in medium bowl; beat until well blended. Stir in *1 cup* coconut, nuts and morsels.

SPREAD mixture evenly over base; sprinkle with *remaining* coconut. Bake for 28 to 30 minutes or until center is almost set (center will firm when cool). Cool in pan on wire rack.   *Makes 24 squares*

Choco-Scutterbotch

⅔ **CRISCO® Butter Flavor Stick or ⅔ cup CRISCO® Butter Flavor Shortening**
½ **cup firmly packed light brown sugar**
2 **eggs**
1 **package (18.25 ounces package) PILLSBURY® Moist Supreme® Classic Yellow Cake Mix**
1 **cup toasted rice cereal**
½ **cup butterscotch chips**
½ **cup milk chocolate chunks**
½ **cup semisweet chocolate chips**
½ **cup coarsely chopped walnuts or pecans**

1. Heat oven to 375°F. Place sheets of foil on countertop for cooling cookies.

2. Combine ⅔ cup CRISCO Shortening and brown sugar in large bowl. Beat at medium speed of electric mixer until well blended. Beat in eggs.

3. Add cake mix gradually at low speed. Mix until well blended. Stir in cereal, butterscotch chips, chocolate chunks, chocolate chips and nuts. Stir until well blended.

4. Shape dough into 1¼-inch balls. Place 2 inches apart on ungreased baking sheet. Flatten slightly. Shape sides to form circle, if necessary.

5. Bake for 7 to 9 minutes or until lightly browned around edges. *Do not overbake.* Cool 2 minutes on baking sheet. Remove cookies to foil to cool completely. *Makes 3 dozen cookies*

Moon Rocks

1 package (18¼ ounces) devil's food or German chocolate
    cake mix with pudding in the mix
3 eggs
½ cup (1 stick) butter, melted
2 cups slightly crushed (2½-inch) pretzel sticks
1½ cups uncooked old-fashioned oats
1 cup swirled chocolate and white chocolate chips or
    candy-coated semisweet chocolate baking pieces

1. Preheat oven to 350°F. Combine cake mix, eggs and butter in large bowl. Stir in pretzels, oats and chocolate chips. (Dough will be stiff.)

2. Drop dough by rounded teaspoonfuls about 2 inches apart onto ungreased cookie sheets.

3. Bake 7 to 9 minutes or until set. Let cookies cool on cookie sheets 1 minute; transfer to wire racks to to cool completely.

Makes 60 cookies

Chocolate Chip-Oat Cookies

1 package (18¼ ounces) yellow cake mix
1 teaspoon baking powder
¾ cup vegetable oil
2 eggs
1 teaspoon vanilla
1 cup uncooked old-fashioned oats
¾ cup semisweet chocolate chips

1. Preheat oven to 350°F. Lightly grease cookie sheets or line with parchment paper.

2. Stir together cake mix and baking powder in large bowl. Add oil, eggs and vanilla; beat by hand until well blended. Stir in oats and chocolate chips.

3. Drop dough by slightly rounded tablespoonfuls 2 inches apart onto prepared cookie sheets. Bake 10 minutes or until golden brown. *Do not overbake.*

4. Let cookies stand on cookie sheets 5 minutes; tranfer to wire racks to cool completely. *Makes 4 dozen cookies*

Quick Fruit & Lemon Drops

½ cup sugar
1 package (18¼ ounces) lemon cake mix
⅓ cup water
¼ cup (½ stick) butter, softened
1 egg
1 tablespoon grated lemon peel
1 cup mixed dried fruit bits

1. Preheat oven to 350°F. Grease cookie sheets. Place sugar in shallow bowl.

2. Beat cake mix, water, butter, egg and lemon peel in large bowl with electric mixer at low speed until well blended. Beat in fruit bits just until blended.

3. Shape dough by heaping tablespoons into balls; roll in sugar to coat. Place 2 inches apart on prepared cookie sheets.

4. Bake 12 to 14 minutes or until set. Let cookies stand on cookie sheets 2 minutes; transfer to wire racks to cool completely.

Makes about 2 dozen cookies

Note: If dough is too sticky to handle, add about ¼ cup all-purpose flour.

Chocolate and Oat Toffee Bars

¾ cup (1½ sticks) plus 2 tablespoons butter, softened, divided
1 package (18¼ ounces) yellow cake mix with pudding in the mix
2 cups uncooked quick-cooking oats
¼ cup packed brown sugar
1 egg
½ teaspoon vanilla
1 cup toffee chips
½ cup chopped pecans
⅓ cup semisweet chocolate chips

1. Preheat oven to 350°F. Grease 13×9-inch baking pan.

2. Beat ¾ cup butter in large bowl with electric mixer until creamy. Add cake mix, oats, brown sugar, egg and vanilla; beat 1 minute or until well blended. Stir in toffee chips and pecans. Pat dough into prepared pan.

3. Bake 31 to 35 minutes or until golden brown. Remove from oven and cool completely in pan on wire rack.

4. Melt remaining 2 tablespoons butter and chocolate chips in small saucepan over very low heat. Drizzle warm glaze over bars. Let glaze set 1 hour at room temperature. Cut into bars with sharp knife.

Makes 30 bars

Peanut Butter
Cheesecake Bars

1 package (18¼ ounces) yellow cake mix with pudding in the mix
½ cup (1 stick) butter, softened, cut into small pieces
2 packages (8 ounces each) cream cheese, softened
1 cup chunky peanut butter
3 eggs
1¼ cups sugar
1 cup salted roasted peanuts
Melted chocolate (optional)

1. Preheat oven to 325°F. Combine cake mix and butter in large bowl; beat with electric mixer at medium speed just until crumbly. Remove 1 cup mixture. Press remaining mixture evenly into ungreased 13×9-inch baking pan to form crust. Bake 10 minutes; cool on wire rack.

2. Combine cream cheese and peanut butter in large bowl; beat with electric mixer at medium speed until fluffy. Beat in eggs, one at a time, scraping down side of bowl occasionally. Gradually beat in sugar until light. Spoon filling over cooled crust.

3. Combine reserved cake mix mixture and peanuts; sprinkle evenly over filling.

4. Bake 45 minutes or until cake is just set and knife inserted into center comes out clean. Remove from oven; cool at room temperature 30 minutes. Chill at least 2 hours before serving. Drizzle with melted chocolate, if desired. *Makes 24 servings*

Crispy Thumbprint Cookies

Prep and Cook Time: 30 minutes

1 package (18¼ ounces) yellow cake mix
½ cup vegetable oil
¼ cup water
1 egg
3 cups crisp rice cereal, crushed
½ cup chopped walnuts
6 tablespoons raspberry or strawberry preserves

1. Preheat oven to 375°F.

2. Combine cake mix, oil, water and egg in large bowl. Beat at medium speed with electric mixer until well blended. Add cereal and walnuts; mix until well blended.

3. Drop by heaping teaspoonfuls about 2 inches apart onto ungreased baking sheets. Use thumb to make indentation in each cookie. Spoon about ½ teaspoon preserves into center of each cookie.

4. Bake 9 to 11 minutes or until golden brown. Cool cookies 1 minute on baking sheets; remove from baking sheets to wire racks to cool completely.   *Makes 3 dozen cookies*

Granola Raisin Bars

1 package (18¼ ounces) yellow cake mix with pudding in the mix, divided
½ cup (1 stick) butter, melted, divided
1 egg
4 cups granola cereal with raisins

1. Preheat oven to 350°F. Lightly spray 13×9-inch baking pan with nonstick cooking spray. Reserve ½ cup cake mix; set aside.

2. Combine remaining cake mix, 4 tablespoons butter and egg in large bowl; stir until well blended. (Dough will be thick and sticky.) Spoon dough into prepared pan. Cover with plastic wrap and press dough evenly into pan, using plastic wrap to keep hands from sticking to dough.

3. Bake 8 minutes. Meanwhile, combine reserved cake mix, granola cereal and remaining 4 tablespoons butter in medium bowl; stir until well blended. Spread mixture evenly over partially baked dough.

4. Return pan to oven; bake 15 to 20 minutes or until edges are lightly browned. Cool completely on wire rack. *Makes 15 bars*

Buried Cherry
Bars

1 jar (10 ounces) maraschino cherries
1 package (18¼ ounces) devil's food cake mix *without*
pudding in the mix
1 cup (2 sticks) butter, melted
1 egg
½ teaspoon almond extract
1½ cups semisweet chocolate chips
¾ cup sweetened condensed milk
½ cup chopped pecans

1. Preheat oven to 350°F. Lightly grease 13×9-inch baking pan. Drain maraschino cherries, reserving 2 tablespoons juice. Cut cherries into quarters.

2. Combine cake mix, butter, egg and almond extract in large bowl; mix well. (Batter will be very thick.) Spread batter in prepared pan. Lightly press cherries into batter.

3. Combine chocolate chips and sweetened condensed milk in small saucepan. Cook over low heat, stirring constantly, until chocolate melts. Stir in reserved cherry juice. Spread chocolate mixture over cherries in pan; sprinkle with pecans.

4. Bake 35 minutes or until almost set in center. Cool completely on wire rack. *Makes 24 bars*

Pastel Mint Swirls

⅓ cup coarse or granulated sugar
**1 package (18¼ ounces) devil's food cake mix *without*
    pudding in the mix**
3 eggs
¼ cup butter, melted
¼ cup unsweetened cocoa powder
144 small *or* 48 large pastel mint chips

1. Preheat oven to 375°F. Place sugar in shallow bowl.

2. Combine cake mix, eggs, butter and cocoa in large bowl just until blended. (Dough will be stiff.)

3. Shape dough into 1-inch balls; roll in sugar to coat. Place 2 inches apart on ungreased cookie sheets.

4. Bake 8 to 9 minutes or until tops are cracked. Gently press 3 small or 1 large mint into top of each cookie. Let cookies stand on cookie sheet 1 minute; transfer to wire racks to cool completely.   *Makes 48 cookies*

Sunshine Sandwiches

⅓ cup coarse or granulated sugar

¾ cup (1½ sticks) plus 2 tablespoons butter, softened, divided

1 egg

2 tablespoons grated lemon peel

1 package (18¼ ounces) lemon cake mix with pudding in the mix

¼ cup yellow cornmeal

2 cups sifted powdered sugar

2 to 3 tablespoons lemon juice

2 drops yellow food coloring (optional)

1. Preheat oven to 375°F. Place coarse sugar in shallow bowl.

2. Beat ¾ cup butter in large bowl with electric mixer at medium speed until fluffy. Add egg and lemon peel; beat 30 seconds. Add cake mix, ⅓ at a time, beating at low speed after each addition until combined. Stir in cornmeal. (Dough will be stiff.)

3. Shape dough into 1-inch balls; roll in sugar to coat. Place 2 inches apart on ungreased cookie sheets.

4. Bake 8 to 9 minutes or until bottoms begin to brown. Let cookies stand on cookie sheets 1 minute; transfer to wire racks to cool completely.

5. Meanwhile, beat powdered sugar and remaining 2 tablespoons butter in small bowl with electric mixer at low speed until blended. Gradually add enough lemon juice to reach spreading consistency. Stir in food coloring, if desired.

6. Spread 1 slightly rounded teaspoon frosting on bottom of one cookie. Top with second cookie, bottom side down. Repeat with remaining cookies and frosting. Store covered at room temperature for up to 24 hours or freeze. *Makes 30 cookies*

Dark Chocolate Lava Cakes (p. 98)   **Candy Bar Cake (p. 97)**

Fudgy Ripple Cake (p. 96)   Fudgy Banana Oat Cake (p. 107)

Chocolate Lovers

Chocolate Lovers' Cake

1 package (18¼ ounces) chocolate cake mix, plus ingredients to prepare mix
3 tablespoons seedless raspberry preserves, melted
   Chocolate Ganache (recipe follows)
⅔ cup sweetened condensed milk
1 cup (6 ounces) semisweet chocolate chips
1 tablespoon butter
   Chocolate Shapes (recipe follows, optional)

1. Prepare and bake cake mix according to package directions for two 8- or 9-inch layers. Do not cool completely. Remove cakes from pans. Poke holes all over top of each layer with toothpick. Brush melted preserves over warm cake layers. Set aside to cool completely.

2. Prepare Chocolate Ganache. While ganache cools, combine sweetened condensed milk, chocolate chips and butter in small heavy saucepan. Cook over low heat until chips are melted and mixture is smooth. Cool slightly.

3. Place one cake layer on serving plate; spread sweetened condensed milk mixture evenly over cake. Top with second cake layer. Frost cake with Chocolate Ganache; top with Chocolate Shapes, if desired.

Makes 12 servings

Chocolate Ganache: Combine ¾ cup heavy cream, 1 tablespoon butter and 1 tablespoon granulated sugar in small saucepan; bring to a boil over high heat, stirring until sugar is dissolved. Place 1½ cups semisweet chocolate chips in medium bowl. Pour cream mixture over chocolate; let stand 5 minutes. Stir until smooth; let stand 15 minutes or until ganache reaches desired consistency. (Ganache will thicken as it cools.) Makes about 1½ cups.

Chocolate Shapes: Place sheet of waxed paper onto inverted baking sheet. Place ⅓ cup chocolate chips in resealable plastic food storage bag; microwave on HIGH 1 minute. Knead bag. Microwave additional 10 to 20 seconds until chocolate is melted and smooth. Cut off tiny corner of bag. Pipe chocolate in desired shapes onto waxed paper. Let stand in cool, dry place until chocolate is set. (Do not refrigerate.) When chocolate is set, gently peel shapes off waxed paper.

Elegant Chocolate Angel Torte

Prep Time: 30 minutes • **Bake Time:** 45 minutes • **Cool Time:** 2 hours

⅓ cup HERSHEY'S Cocoa
1 package (about 16 ounces) angel food cake mix
2 envelopes (1.3 ounces each) dry whipped topping mix
1 cup cold nonfat milk
1 teaspoon vanilla extract
1 cup strawberry purée*
Strawberries

Mash 2 cups sliced fresh strawberries (or frozen berries, thawed) in blender or food processor. Cover; blend until smooth. Purée should measure 1 cup.

1. Move oven rack to lowest position.

2. Sift cocoa over dry cake mix in large bowl; stir to blend. Proceed with mixing cake as directed on package. Bake and cool as directed for 10-inch tube pan. Carefully run knife along side of pan to loosen cake; remove from pan. Using serrated knife, slice cake horizontally into four layers.

3. Prepare whipped topping mix as directed on package, using 1 cup nonfat milk and 1 teaspoon vanilla. Fold in strawberry purée.

4. Place bottom cake layer on serving plate; spread with ¼ of strawberry topping. Set next cake layer on top; spread with ¼ of topping. Continue layering cake and topping. Garnish with strawberries. Refrigerate until ready to serve. Slice cake with sharp serrated knife, cutting with gentle sawing motion. Cover; refrigerate leftover cake.

Makes about 16 servings

Sinfully Simple Chocolate Cake

**1 package (18¼ ounces) chocolate cake mix, plus
    ingredients to prepare mix**
1 cup whipping cream, chilled
⅓ cup chocolate syrup
    Fresh fruit for garnish (optional)

1. Prepare cake mix according to package directions for two 8- or 9-inch layers. Cool completely.

2. Beat whipping cream in medium bowl with electric mixer at high speed until it begins to thicken. Gradually add chocolate syrup; beat until soft peaks form.

3. To assemble, place one cake layer on serving plate; spread with half of chocolate whipped cream. Place second cake layer on top; spread top and side with remaining chocolate whipped cream. Garnish, if desired. Store in refrigerator.   *Makes 12 servings*

Rocky Road Cake

1 cup chopped walnuts or dry roasted peanuts
1 package (18¼ ounces) devil's food cake mix
1⅓ cups water
3 eggs
½ cup vegetable oil
2 teaspoons instant coffee granules (optional)
4 cups miniature marshmallows
1 jar (16 ounces) hot fudge topping

1. Preheat oven to 350°F. Grease bottom of 13×9-inch baking pan; set aside.

2. Place 10-inch skillet over medium high heat until hot. Add walnuts; cook 3 to 4 minutes or until just brown, stirring frequently. Remove from heat; set aside.

3. Beat cake mix, water, eggs, oil, and coffee granules, if desired, in large bowl with electric mixer at low speed 1 minute or until well blended. Pour evenly into prepared pan.

4. Bake 33 minutes or until toothpick inserted into center comes out almost clean. Remove from oven to wire rack. Immediately sprinkle marshmallows, then walnuts evenly over cake. Let stand 15 minutes.

5. Meanwhile, heat fudge topping in microwave according to jar directions. Drizzle syrup evenly over cake. Cool completely.

Makes 16 servings

Fudgy Ripple Cake

**1 package (18.25 ounces) yellow cake mix plus ingredients
to prepare mix**
1 package (3 ounces) cream cheese, softened
2 tablespoons unsweetened cocoa powder
Fudgy Glaze (recipe follows)
½ cup "M&M's"® Chocolate Mini Baking Bits

Preheat oven to 350°F. Lightly grease and flour 10-inch Bundt or ring pan; set aside. Prepare cake mix as package directs. In medium bowl combine 1½ cups prepared batter, cream cheese and cocoa powder until smooth. Pour half of yellow batter into prepared pan. Drop spoonfuls of chocolate batter over yellow batter in pan. Top with remaining yellow batter. Bake about 45 minutes or until toothpick inserted near center comes out clean. Cool completely on wire rack. Unmold cake onto serving plate. Prepare Fudgy Glaze; spread over top of cake, allowing some glaze to run over side. Sprinkle with "M&M's"® Chocolate Mini Baking Bits. Store in tightly covered container. *Makes 10 servings*

Fudgy Glaze

1 square (1 ounce) semi-sweet chocolate
1 cup powdered sugar
⅓ cup unsweetened cocoa powder
3 tablespoons milk
½ teaspoon vanilla extract

Place chocolate in small microwave-safe bowl. Microwave at HIGH 30 seconds; stir. Repeat as necessary until chocolate is completely melted, stirring at 10-second intervals; set aside. In medium bowl combine powdered sugar and cocoa powder. Stir in milk, vanilla and melted chocolate until smooth.

Candy Bar Cake

1 package (18¼ ounces) devil's food cake mix *without* pudding in the mix

1 cup sour cream

4 eggs

⅓ cup vegetable oil

¼ cup water

3 containers (16 ounces each) white frosting

1 bar (2.1 ounces) chocolate-covered crispy peanut butter candy, chopped

1 bar (2.07 ounces) chocolate-covered peanut, caramel and nougat candy, chopped

1 bar (1.4 ounces) chocolate-covered toffee candy, chopped

4 bars (1.55 ounces each) milk chocolate

1. Preheat oven to 350°F. Grease and flour two 9-inch round baking pans.

2. Beat cake mix, sour cream, eggs, oil and water in large bowl with electric mixer at low speed about 1 minute or until blended. Increase speed to medium; beat 1 to 2 minutes or until smooth. Spread batter in prepared pans.

3. Bake 30 to 35 minutes or until toothpick inserted into centers comes out clean. Cool in pans on wire racks 10 minutes; remove from pans and cool completely on wire racks.

4. Cut each cake layer in half horizontally. Place 1 cake layer on serving plate. Spread generously with frosting. Sprinkle with 1 chopped candy bar. Repeat with 2 more cake layers, additional frosting and remaining 2 chopped candy bars. Top with remaining cake layer; frost top of cake with remaining frosting.

5. Break milk chocolate bars into pieces along score lines. Stand chocolate pieces in frosting around outside edge of cake as shown in photo (page 86). *Makes 12 servings*

Dark Chocolate Lava Cakes

1½ cups cold milk
1 package (4-serving size) instant chocolate pudding and pie filling mix
1 package (18¼ ounces) dark chocolate cake mix
1 cup buttermilk
2 whole eggs
3 egg yolks
¼ cup vegetable oil
2 tablespoons water
1 tablespoon butter, melted
¼ cup granulated sugar
Sifted powdered sugar

1. Combine milk and pudding mix in medium bowl; whisk until smooth. Place plastic wrap on surface of pudding; refrigerate.

2. Combine cake mix, buttermilk, whole eggs, egg yolks, oil and water in large bowl; stir by hand until almost smooth (a few lumps will remain). *Do not use electric mixer.* Cover and refrigerate batter 1 hour.

3. Preheat oven to 400°F. Brush melted butter inside 14 (5-ounce) ramekins. Sprinkle evenly with granulated sugar.

4. Place 2 tablespoons batter into each prepared ramekin. Bake 10 to 12 minutes (batter will not cook through completely). Remove ramekins from oven; place 1 heaping tablespoon pudding in center of each ramekin and cover with additional 2 tablespoons batter.

5. Bake 14 to 16 minutes until wooden pick inserted in top layer of cakes comes out clean. Remove from oven to wire racks; cool 7 to 10 minutes. Invert cakes onto serving plates. Sprinkle with powdered sugar. Serve immediately. *Makes 14 cakes*

Chocolate Cream Torte

1 package DUNCAN HINES® Moist Deluxe® Devil's Food Cake Mix
1 package (8 ounces) cream cheese, softened
½ cup sugar
1 teaspoon vanilla extract
1 cup finely chopped pecans
1 cup whipping cream, chilled
Strawberry halves for garnish
Mint leaves for garnish

1. Preheat oven to 350°F. Grease and flour two 8- or 9-inch round cake pans.

2. Prepare, bake and cool cakes following package directions for basic recipe. Chill layers for ease in splitting.

3. Place cream cheese, sugar and vanilla extract in small bowl. Beat at low speed with electric mixer until smooth. Add pecans; stir until blended. Set aside. Beat whipping cream in small bowl until stiff peaks form. Fold whipped cream into cream cheese mixture.

4. To assemble, split each cake layer in half horizontally (see Tip). Place one cake layer on serving plate. Spread top with one fourth of filling. Repeat with remaining layers and filling. Garnish with strawberry halves and mint leaves, if desired. Refrigerate until ready to serve.

Makes 12 to 16 servings

Tip: To split layers evenly, measure cake with ruler. Divide into 2 equal layers. Mark with toothpicks. Cut through layers with serrated knife, using toothpicks as guide.

Decadent Chocolate Delight

1 package (18¼ ounces) chocolate cake mix
1 cup (8 ounces) sour cream
1 cup chocolate chips
1 cup water
4 eggs
¾ cup vegetable oil
**1 package (4-serving size) instant chocolate pudding and
     pie filling mix**
   Ice cream (optional)

Slow Cooker Directions

1. Grease slow cooker.

2. Combine cake mix, sour cream, chips, water, eggs, oil and pudding and pie filling mix in slow cooker; mix well.

3. Cover; cook on LOW 6 to 8 hours or on HIGH 3 to 4 hours. Serve hot or warm with ice cream.   *Makes 12 servings*

Polka Dot Cake

1 package (18¼ ounces) chocolate cake mix, plus ingredients to prepare mix
¾ cup white chocolate chips
2 bars (3½ ounces each) good-quality bittersweet or semisweet chocolate, broken into small pieces
¼ cup (½ stick) butter, cut into small chunks
¼ cup heavy cream
1 tablespoon powdered sugar
Dash salt
¼ cup small chocolate nonpareil candies

1. Preheat oven to 350°F. Generously spray 12-cup bundt pan with nonstick cooking spray.

2. Prepare cake mix according to package directions. Pour batter into prepared pan; sprinkle with chips.

3. Bake 40 minutes or until toothpick inserted near center comes out clean. Cool cake in pan on wire rack 30 minutes; invert cake onto wire rack and cool completely. Place sheet of waxed paper under wire rack.

4. Combine chocolate, butter, cream, powdered sugar and salt in small, heavy saucepan. Heat over very low heat, stirring constantly, just until butter and chocolate melt. Mixture should be tepid, not hot. Immediately spoon chocolate glaze over cake, spreading to cover side as well as top. Scoop up any glaze from waxed paper and spoon over cake.

5. Arrange nonpareil candies over glaze. Let glaze set about 2 hours at room temperature. Do not refrigerate. *Makes 16 servings*

Fudgy Banana Oat Cake

Topping

> 1 cup QUAKER® Oats (quick or old fashioned, uncooked)
> ½ cup firmly packed brown sugar
> ¼ cup (½ stick) margarine or butter, chilled

Filling

> 1 cup (6 ounces) semisweet chocolate pieces
> ⅔ cup sweetened condensed milk (not evaporated milk)
> 1 tablespoon margarine or butter

Cake

> 1 package (18.25 ounces) devil's food cake mix
> 1¼ cups mashed ripe bananas (about 3 large)
> ⅓ cup vegetable oil
> 3 eggs
> Banana slices (optional)
> Sweetened whipped cream (optional)

Heat oven to 350°F. Lightly grease bottom only of 13×9-inch baking pan. For topping, combine oats and brown sugar. Cut in margarine until mixture is crumbly; set aside.

For filling, in small saucepan, heat chocolate pieces, sweetened condensed milk and margarine over low heat until chocolate is melted, stirring occasionally. Remove from heat; set aside.

For cake, in large mixing bowl, combine cake mix, bananas, oil and eggs. Blend at low speed of electric mixer until dry ingredients are moistened. Beat at medium speed 2 minutes. Spread batter evenly into prepared pan. Drop chocolate filling by teaspoonfuls evenly over batter. Sprinkle with reserved oat topping. Bake 40 to 45 minutes or until cake pulls away from sides of pan and topping is golden brown. Cool cake in pan on wire rack. Cut into squares. Garnish with banana slices and sweetened whipped cream, if desired. *Makes 15 servings*

**Peanut Butter & Milk
Chocolate Cupcakes (p. 132)**

Rainbow Cake (p. 119)

ce Cream Sandwiches (p. 118)   Jam Jam Bars (p. 133)

Kids' Konfections

Garbage Pail Cookies

1 package (18¼ ounces) white cake mix with pudding in the mix
½ cup (1 stick) butter, softened
2 eggs
1 teaspoon vanilla
1 teaspoon ground cinnamon
½ cup mini candy-coated chocolate pieces
½ cup salted peanuts
½ cup peanut butter chips
1½ cups crushed salted potato chips

1. Preheat oven to 350°F. Lightly grease cookie sheets.

2. Beat half of cake mix, butter, eggs, vanilla and cinnamon in large bowl with electric mixer at medium speed until light and fluffy. Beat in remaining cake mix until well blended. Stir in candy-coated chocolate pieces, peanuts and peanut butter chips. Stir in potato chips. (Dough will be stiff.)

3. Drop batter by rounded tablespoonfuls 2 inches apart onto prepared cookie sheets.

4. Bake 15 minutes or until golden brown. Let cookies stand on cookie sheets 2 minutes; transfer to wire racks to cool completely.

Makes 40 cookies

Chocolate Peanut Butter Candy Bars

1 package (18¼ ounces) devil's food or dark chocolate cake mix *without* pudding in the mix
1 can (5 ounces) evaporated milk
⅓ cup butter, melted
½ cup dry-roasted peanuts
4 packages (1½ ounces each) chocolate peanut butter cups, coarsely chopped

1. Preheat oven to 350°F. Lightly grease 13×9-inch baking pan.

2. Combine cake mix, evaporated milk and butter in large bowl; beat with electric mixer at medium speed until well blended. (Dough will be stiff.) Spread ⅔ of dough in prepared pan. Sprinkle with peanuts.

3. Bake 10 minutes; remove from oven and sprinkle with chopped candy.

4. Drop remaining dough by large spoonfuls over candy. Bake 15 to 20 minutes or until set. Cool completely on wire rack.

Makes 24 servings

Hidden Surprise Cake

1 package (16 ounces) angel food cake mix, plus ingredients to prepare mix
1½ to 2 pints chocolate ice cream, softened
2 cups whipping cream, well chilled
¼ cup unsweetened cocoa powder
6 tablespoons powdered sugar
2 to 4 tablespoons mini chocolate chips (optional)

1. Prepare, bake and cool angel food cake according to package directions.

2. Beat cream and cocoa in large bowl with electric mixer at medium speed until slightly thickened. Gradually beat in powdered sugar at high speed until stiff peaks form, set aside.

3. Place cake on work surface. Using serrated knife, cut horizontally across cake 1 inch from top. Remove top of cake; set aside. Scoop out inside of cake with hands, leaving 1 inch shell on side and bottom. (Be careful not to tear through cake.) Spoon ice cream into cake, packing down. Cover with cake top.

4. Frost top and side of cake with chocolate whipped cream. Sprinkle with chocolate chips, if desired. Serve immediately.

Makes 12 servings

Note: The cake can be prepared and filled, without frosting, up to one week in advance. Wrap in heavy-duty foil and store in the freezer. Remove 15 minutes before frosting. Serve immediately after frosting.

Marshmallow Fudge Sundae Cupcakes

1 package (18¼ ounces) chocolate cake mix, plus ingredients to prepare mix
2 packages (4 ounces each) waffle bowls
40 marshmallows
1 jar (8 ounces) hot fudge topping
1¼ cups whipped topping
¼ cup colored sprinkles
1 jar (10 ounces) maraschino cherries

1. Preheat oven to 350°F. Lightly spray 20 standard (2½-inch) muffin pan cups with nonstick cooking spray.

2. Prepare cake mix according to package directions. Spoon batter into prepared cups, filling ⅔ full.

3. Bake about 20 minutes or until toothpicks inserted into centers come out clean. Cool in pans on wire racks about 10 minutes.

4. Remove cupcakes from pans and place one cupcake in each waffle bowl. Place waffle bowls on baking sheets. Top each cupcake with 2 marshmallows and return to oven for 2 minutes or until marshmallows are slightly softened.

5. Remove lid from fudge topping; heat in microwave at HIGH 10 seconds or until softened. Spoon 2 teaspoons fudge topping over each cupcake. Top with 1 tablespoon whipped topping, sprinkles and cherry.

Makes 20 cupcakes

Ice Cream Sandwiches

1 package (18¼ ounces) chocolate cake mix with pudding in the mix
2 eggs
¼ cup warm water
3 tablespoons butter, melted
1 pint vanilla ice cream, softened
   Colored decorating sugar or sprinkles
   Powdered sugar (optional)

1. Preheat oven to 350°F. Lightly spray 13×9-inch pan with nonstick cooking spray. Line pan with foil and spray foil.

2. Beat cake mix, eggs, water and melted butter in large bowl with electric mixer until well blended. (Dough will be thick and sticky.) Spoon dough into prepared pan. Cover with plastic wrap and press dough evenly into pan, using plastic wrap to keep hands from sticking to dough. Remove plastic wrap and prick surface all over with fork (about 40 times) to prevent dough from rising too much.

3. Bake 20 minutes or until toothpick inserted into center comes out clean. Cool in pan on wire rack.

4. Cut cookie in half crosswise; remove one half from pan. Spread ice cream evenly over cookie half remaining in pan. Top with second half; use foil in pan to wrap up sandwich.

5. Freeze at least 4 hours. Cut into 8 equal pieces; dip cut ends in sugar or sprinkles. Wrap and freeze sandwiches until ready to serve. Sprinkle with powdered sugar before serving, if desired.   *Makes 8 sandwiches*

Peppermint Ice Cream Sandwiches: Stir ⅓ cup crushed peppermint candies into vanilla ice cream before assembling. Dip ends of sandwiches in additional crushed peppermint candies to coat.

Tip: If the ice cream is too hard to scoop easily, microwave on HIGH 10 seconds to soften.

Rainbow Cake

**1 (18¼ ounces) cake mix, any flavor, plus ingredients to
   prepare mix**
⅓ cup raspberry jam
1 container (16 ounces) vanilla frosting
Multi-colored coated fruit candies

1. Prepare cake according to package directions and bake in 17×11-inch jelly-roll pan. Remove from oven; cool in pan completely.

2. Using knife or square cookie cutter, cut 15 (2½ inch) squares from cake. Spread raspberry jam on 1 layer. Top with second cake layer and spread with jam. Top with third cake layer.

3. Frost entire cake with vanilla frosting. Repeat to make 5 cakes. Sprinkle with candies or decorate as desired.   *Makes 5 cakes*

Note: For easy icing application, brush crumbs off cake layers. Then apply a first thin layer "crumb coat" of icing on cake. Place cake in freezer for about 20 minutes. Then apply the second, decorative frosting layer to top and sides of cake.

S'More Snack Cake

1 package (18¼ ounces) yellow cake mix, plus ingredients to prepare mix
1 cup chocolate chunks, divided
1½ cups miniature marshmallows
1 cup bear-shaped graham crackers (honey or chocolate flavor)

1. Preheat oven to 350°F. Grease 13×9-inch baking pan.

2. Prepare cake mix according to package directions. Spread batter in prepared pan. Sprinkle with ½ cup chocolate chunks.

3. Bake 30 minutes. Remove cake from oven; sprinkle with remaining ½ cup chocolate chunks and marshmallows. Arrange bears evenly over top of cake as shown in photo.

4. Return cake to oven; bake 8 minutes or until marshmallows are golden brown. Cool completely before cutting.   *Makes 24 servings*

Note: This cake is best served the day it is made.

Mini Doughnut Cupcakes

1 cup sugar
1½ teaspoons ground cinnamon
1 package (18¼ ounces) yellow or white cake mix, plus ingredients to prepare mix
1 tablespoon ground nutmeg

1. Preheat oven to 350°F. Grease and flour 24 mini (1¾-inch) muffin pan cups. Combine sugar and cinnamon in small bowl; set aside.

2. Prepare cake mix according to package directions; stir nutmeg into batter. Fill prepared muffin cups ⅔ full.

3. Bake about 12 minutes or until lightly browned and toothpick inserted into centers comes out clean.

4. Remove cupcakes from pans; roll in cinnamon-sugar mixture until completely coated. Serve warm or at room temperature.

Makes about 48 cupcakes

Tip: Save any remaining cinnamon-sugar mixture to sprinkle on toast and pancakes.

PB & J Sandwich Cake

1 package (18¼ ounces) white cake mix, plus ingredients to prepare mix
¾ cup powdered sugar
5 tablespoons peanut butter
2 to 3 tablespoons whipping cream or milk
1 tablespoon butter, softened
½ cup strawberry or grape jam

1. Preheat oven to 350°F. Grease two 8-inch square baking pans. Prepare cake mix according to package directions. Spread batter in prepared pans.

2. Bake 30 minutes or until toothpick inserted into centers comes out clean. Cool in pans on wire racks 30 minutes; remove from pans and cool completely on wire racks.

3. Carefully slice off browned tops of both cakes to create flat, even layers. Place 1 layer on serving plate, cut side up.

4. Beat powdered sugar, peanut butter, 2 tablespoons cream and butter with electric mixer at medium speed until light and creamy. Add remaining 1 tablespoon cream if necessary to reach spreading consistency. Gently spread filling over cut side of cake layer on serving plate. Spread jam over peanut butter filling. Top with second cake layer, cut side up.

5. Cut cake in half diagonally to resemble sandwich. To serve, cut into thin slices across the diagonal using serrated knife.   *Makes 12 servings*

Flapjack
Party Stack

**1 package (18¼ ounces) yellow cake mix, plus ingredients
    to prepare mix**
1 container (16 ounces) vanilla frosting
1 quart fresh strawberries, washed, hulled and sliced
1 cup caramel or butterscotch ice cream topping

1. Preheat oven to 350°F. Grease bottoms and sides of four 9-inch round cake pans; line pans with waxed paper. Prepare and bake cake mix according to package directions. Let cakes cool in pans on wire racks 15 minutes. Remove from pans; cool completely.

2. Reserve ¼ cup frosting. Place 1 cake layer on serving plate; spread or pipe ⅓ of remaining frosting in swirls on cake to resemble whipped butter. Top with sliced strawberries. Repeat with next 2 cake layers, frosting and strawberries. Top stack with remaining cake layer.

3. Warm caramel topping in microwave just until pourable. Drizzle over cake. Spread or pipe remaining ¼ cup frosting in center; garnish with remaining strawberries. *Makes 12 servings*

Carrot
Snack Cake

1 package (18¼ ounces) butter recipe yellow cake mix with pudding in the mix, plus ingredients to prepare mix
2 jars (4 ounces each) strained carrot baby food
1½ cups chopped walnuts, divided
1 cup shredded carrots
½ cup golden raisins
1½ teaspoons ground cinnamon
1½ teaspoons vanilla, divided
1 package (8 ounces) cream cheese, softened
Grated peel of 1 lemon
2 teaspoons fresh lemon juice
3 cups powdered sugar

1. Preheat oven to 350°F. Grease 13×9-inch baking pan.

2. Prepare cake mix according to package directions using only ½ cup water instead of amount directions call for. Stir carrot baby food, 1 cup walnuts, carrots, raisins, cinnamon and ½ teaspoon vanilla into batter. Spread in prepared pan.

3. Bake 40 minutes or until cake begins to pull away from sides of pan and toothpick inserted into center comes out clean. Cool completely in pan on wire rack.

4. Beat cream cheese in large bowl with electric mixer until fluffy. Beat in lemon peel, lemon juice and remaining 1 teaspoon vanilla. Gradually add powdered sugar, scraping down side of bowl occasionally; beat until well blended and smooth. Spread frosting over cooled cake; sprinkle with remaining ½ cup walnuts. Refrigerate 2 hours before cutting.

Makes 24 servings

Lazy Daisy Cupcakes

1 package (18¼ ounces) yellow cake mix, plus ingredients to prepare mix
Yellow food coloring
1 container (16 ounces) vanilla frosting
30 large marshmallows
24 small round candies or gumdrops

1. Line 24 standard (2½-inch) muffin pan cups with paper liners or spray with nonstick cooking spray. Prepare and bake cake mix in prepared muffin cups according to package directions. Cool in pans on wire racks 15 minutes. Remove cupcakes to racks; cool completely.

2. Add food coloring to frosting, a few drops at a time, until desired color is reached. Frost cooled cupcakes with tinted frosting.

3. Cut each marshmallow crosswise into 4 pieces with scissors. Stretch pieces into petal shapes; place 5 pieces on each cupcake to form flower. Place candy in center of each flower. *Makes 24 cupcakes*

Peanut Butter & Milk Chocolate Cupcakes

1 package (18¼ ounces) butter recipe yellow cake mix with pudding in the mix, plus ingredients to prepare mix

½ cup creamy peanut butter

½ cup (1 stick) unsalted butter, softened, divided

2 bars (3½ ounces each) milk chocolate, broken into small pieces

¼ cup heavy cream

Dash salt

Peanut butter chips (optional)

1. Preheat oven to 350°F. Line 24 standard (2½-inch) muffin pan cups with paper liners.

2. Prepare cake mix according to package directions using ½ cup peanut butter and ¼ cup butter. Fill muffin cups evenly with batter.

3. Bake 24 to 26 minutes or until light golden brown and toothpick inserted into centers comes out clean. Cool cupcakes in pans on wire racks 5 minutes; remove from pans and cool completely on wire racks.

4. Combine chocolate, remaining butter, cream and salt in small, heavy saucepan. Heat over very low heat, stirring constantly, just until butter and chocolate melt. Mixture should be luke warm, not hot. Immediately spoon about 1 tablespoon chocolate glaze over each cupcake, spreading to cover top. Sprinkle with peanut butter chips, if desired.

Makes 24 cupcakes

Jam Jam
Bars

1 package (18¼ ounces) yellow or white cake mix with pudding in the mix
½ cup (1 stick) butter, melted
1 cup apricot preserves or raspberry jam
1 package (11 ounces) peanut butter and milk chocolate chips

1. Preheat oven to 350°F. Lightly spray 13×9-inch baking pan with nonstick cooking spray.

2. Pour cake mix into large bowl; stir in butter until well blended. (Dough will be lumpy.) Remove ½ cup dough and set aside. Press remaining dough evenly into prepared pan. Spread preserves in thin layer over dough in pan.

3. Place chips in medium bowl. Stir in reserved dough until well mixed. (Dough will remain in small lumps evenly distributed throughout chips.) Sprinkle mixture evenly over preserves.

4. Bake 20 minutes or until lightly browned and bubbling at edges. Cool completely in pan on wire rack.   *Makes 24 bars*

**Pretty-in-Pink
Peppermint Cupcakes (p.142)**

Pumpkin Cheesecake Bars (p. 143

Caramel Pecan
Spice Cakes (p.152)

Wolfman Cake (p. 153)

Year-Round Holidays

Chocolate Gingersnaps

¾ **cup sugar**
1 **package (18¼ ounces) chocolate cake mix** *without* **pudding in the mix**
1 **tablespoon ground ginger**
2 **eggs**
⅓ **cup vegetable oil**

1. Preheat oven to 350°F. Spray cookie sheets with nonstick cooking spray. Place sugar into shallow bowl.

2. Combine cake mix and ginger in large bowl. Add eggs and oil; stir until well blended.

3. Shape tablespoonfuls of dough into 1-inch balls; roll in sugar to coat. Place 2 inches apart on prepared cookie sheets.

4. Bake about 10 minutes; transfer to wire racks to cool completely.

Makes about 3 dozen cookies

Magical
Wizard Hats

**1 package (18¼ ounces) cake mix, any flavor, plus
   ingredients to prepare mix
2 containers (16 ounces each) vanilla frosting
   Yellow and purple or black food colorings
2 packages (4 ounces each) sugar cones
   Orange sugar, decors and black decorating gel**

1. Line 24 standard (2½-inch) muffin pan cups with paper baking liners,
or spray with nonstick cooking spray. Prepare and bake cake mix in muffin
pan cups according to package directions. Cool in pans on wire racks
15 minutes. Remove cupcakes to racks; cool completely.

2. Frost cupcakes. Place ½ cup remaining frosting in small bowl; tint with
yellow food coloring. Tint remaining frosting with purple or black food
coloring.

3. Spread sugar cones with dark frosting, covering completely. Place
1 cone upside down on each frosted cupcake. Spoon yellow frosting into
small resealable plastic food storage bag. Cut off small corner of bag; pipe
yellow frosting around base of each frosted cone. Decorate as desired.

Makes 24 cupcakes

Coconut Mother's Day Cake

1 package (18¼ ounces) white cake mix
1 can (about 13 ounces) lite coconut milk
4 egg whites
1 container (16 ounces) vanilla frosting
2 cups flaked coconut
   Violet food coloring paste
   Edible flowers (optional)

1. Preheat oven to 350°F. Grease two 8-inch round cake pans; line with with parchment paper.

2. Combine cake mix, coconut milk and egg whites in large bowl; beat with electric mixer at low speed for 30 seconds. Beat 2 minutes at medium-low speed or until well blended.

3. Divide batter evenly between prepared pans. Bake 40 to 45 minutes or until toothpicks inserted into centers come out clean. Cool in pans on wire racks 10 minutes. Remove from pans to wire racks; cool completely.

4. Place 1 cake layer on cake board or serving platter; frost top with vanilla frosting. Top with remaining layer; frost side and top of cake with remaining frosting.

5. Place coconut in large resealable plastic food storage bag; add small amount of food coloring. Seal bag; knead until coconut is evenly tinted. Press coconut into frosting on side of cake. Garnish with edible flowers, if desired. *Makes 10 servings*

Pretty-in-Pink
Peppermint Cupcakes

1 package (18¼ ounces) white cake mix
1⅓ cups water
3 egg whites
2 tablespoons vegetable oil or melted butter
½ teaspoon peppermint extract
3 to 4 drops red liquid food coloring *or* ¼ teaspoon gel food coloring
1 container (16 ounces) prepared vanilla frosting
½ cup crushed peppermint candies (about 16 candies)

1. Preheat oven to 350°F. Line 30 standard (2½-inch) muffin pan cups with pink or white paper baking cups.

2. Beat cake mix, water, egg whites, oil, peppermint extract and food coloring with electric mixer at low speed 30 seconds. Beat at medium speed 2 minutes.

3. Spoon batter into prepared muffin cups, filling ¾ full. Bake 20 to 22 minutes or until toothpick inserted into centers comes out clean. Cool in pans on wire racks 10 minutes. Remove cupcakes to racks from pans; cool completely on wire racks. (At this point, cupcakes may be frozen up to 3 months. Thaw at room temperature before frosting.)

4. Spread frosting over cooled cupcakes; sprinkle with crushed candies. Store at room temperature up to 24 hours or cover and refrigerate up to 3 days before serving. *Makes 30 cupcakes*

Pumpkin Cheesecake Bars

1 (16-ounce) package pound cake mix
3 eggs, divided
2 tablespoons butter or margarine, melted
4 teaspoons pumpkin pie spice, divided
1 (8-ounce) package cream cheese, softened
**1 (14-ounce) can EAGLE BRAND® Sweetened Condensed Milk
    (NOT evaporated milk)**
1 (15-ounce) can pumpkin (2 cups)
½ teaspoon salt
1 cup chopped nuts

1. Preheat oven to 350°F. In large bowl, beat cake mix, 1 egg, butter and 2 teaspoons pumpkin pie spice until crumbly. Press onto bottom of ungreased 15×10×1-inch baking pan.

2. In large bowl, beat cream cheese until fluffy. Gradually beat in EAGLE BRAND® until smooth. Beat in remaining 2 eggs, pumpkin, remaining 2 teaspoons pumpkin pie spice and salt; mix well. Pour into prepared crust; sprinkle with nuts.

3. Bake 30 to 35 minutes or until set. Cool. Chill; cut into bars. Store leftovers covered in refrigerator.   *Makes 4 dozen bars*

Reindeer Cupcakes

1 package (18¼ ounces) chocolate cake mix, plus
   ingredients to prepare mix
¼ cup (½ stick) butter, softened
4 cups powdered sugar
5 to 6 tablespoons brewed espresso or strong coffee
½ cup (3 ounces) semisweet chocolate chips, melted
1 teaspoon vanilla
   Dash salt
24 pretzel twists, broken in half
   Assorted candies for decoration

1. Preheat oven to 350°F. Line 24 standard (2½-inch) muffin pan cups with paper baking cups.

2. Prepare cake mix according to package directions. Spoon batter into prepared muffin cups, filling ⅔ full. Bake 15 to 20 minutes or until toothpicks inserted into centers come out clean. Cool in pans on wire racks 10 minutes. Remove cupcakes to racks; cool completely.

3. Beat butter in large bowl with electric mixer at medium speed until creamy. Gradually add powdered sugar and 4 tablespoons espresso; beat until smooth. Add melted chocolate, vanilla and salt; beat until well blended. Add remaining espresso, 1 tablespoon at a time, until frosting is of desired spreading consistency.

4. Frost cooled cupcakes with frosting. Decorate with broken pretzel pieces for antlers and assorted candies for reindeer faces.

Makes 24 cupcakes

Ooze Cupcakes

1 package (8 ounces) cream cheese, softened
½ cup powdered sugar
⅓ cup thawed frozen limeade concentrate
1 teaspoon vanilla
   Yellow and blue food coloring
1 package (18¼ ounces) chocolate cake mix, plus
   ingredients to prepare mix
1 egg
   Water and vegetable oil
1 container (16 ounces) vanilla frosting
   Orange sugar

1. Preheat oven to 350°F. Line 24 standard (2½-inch) muffin pan cups with paper liners or spray with nonstick cooking spray.

2. Beat cream cheese, powdered sugar, limeade concentrate and vanilla in large bowl with electric mixer at medium speed until well blended. Tint with yellow food coloring; beat until well blended. Set aside.

3. Prepare cake mix according to package directions using 1 egg, water and oil. Spoon batter into prepared muffin cups, filling half full. Spoon 1 rounded teaspoon cream cheese mixture into center of each cup.

4. Bake about 20 minutes. Cool cupcakes in pans on wire racks 10 minutes; remove from pans and cool completely on wire racks.

5. Add 4 drops yellow food coloring and 2 drops blue food coloring to frosting. Stir until well blended; adjust color as needed by adding additional food coloring 1 drop at a time, blending well after each addition. Spread frosting on cooled cupcakes. Sprinkle with sugar.

Makes 24 cupcakes

Leprechaun Cupcakes

1 package (18¼ ounces) yellow or white cake mix, plus ingredients to prepare mix
1 container (16 ounces) vanilla frosting
  Green, orange and red gumdrops, small candies and black decorating gel

1. Preheat oven to 350°F. Place paper liners in 24 (2½-inch) muffin pan cups. Prepare cake mix according to package directions. Spoon batter into prepared muffin cups, filling ⅔ full.

2. Bake 15 to 20 minutes or until toothpicks inserted into centers come out clean. Cool in pans on wire racks 10 minutes. Remove cupcakes to racks; cool completely.

3. Roll out green gumdrops on generously sugared surface. Cut out pieces to resemble hats. Pipe gel onto hats for hatbands; place candies on hatbands for buckles. Place hats on cupcakes. Roll out orange gumdrops on generously sugared surface. Cut out pieces to resemble sideburns and beards; place on cupcakes. Roll out red gumdrops on generously sugared surface. Cut out small pieces to resemble mouths; place on cupcakes. Place candies on cupcakes for eyes. *Makes 24 cupcakes*

Skull
Cupcakes

1 package (18¼ ounces) cake mix, any flavor
1 egg
  Water
  Vegetable oil
24 small white marshmallows
24 large white marshmallows
  1 container (16 ounces) white frosting
  Black decorating gel
24 black jelly beans, halved
  Black licorice pieces (optional)

1. Preheat oven to 350°F. Place paper liners in 24 (2½-inch) muffin pan cups. Prepare and bake cake mix using egg, water and oil according to package directions. Allow cupcakes to cool completely before decorating.

2. Use an oiled knife or kitchen shears to trim top off 1 small marshmallow. Squeeze cut edge onto base of a large marshmallow to make a rough skull shape as shown in photo. Trim a flat edge on both marshmallows and press flat, sticky side down onto cupcake top. Frost with white frosting, spreading to completely cover marshmallows.

3. Use decorating gel to outline skull shape (see tip). Place 2 jelly bean halves for eyes. Use licorice pieces for nose and mouth, if desired, or draw with decorating gel. Repeat with remaining cupcakes.

Makes 24 cupcakes

Tip: When making the skull outline with piping gel or licorice string, picture the shape of a light bulb.

Caramel Pecan Spice Cakes

Cake

> 1 package DUNCAN HINES® Moist Deluxe® Spice Cake Mix
>
> 1 package (4-serving size) vanilla instant pudding and pie filling mix
>
> 4 eggs
>
> 1 cup water
>
> ⅓ cup vegetable oil
>
> 1½ cups pecan pieces, toasted and finely chopped

Caramel Glaze

> 3 tablespoons butter or margarine
>
> 3 tablespoons brown sugar
>
> 3 tablespoons granulated sugar
>
> 3 tablespoons whipping cream
>
> ½ cup confectioners' sugar
>
> ¼ teaspoon vanilla extract
>
> Pecan halves, for garnish
>
> Maraschino cherry halves, for garnish

1. Preheat oven to 350°F. Grease and flour two 8½×4½×2½-inch loaf pans.

2. For cake, combine cake mix, pudding mix, eggs, water and oil in large bowl. Beat at medium speed with electric mixer for 2 minutes. Stir in toasted pecans. Pour batter into pans. Bake at 350°F for 55 to 60 minutes or until toothpick inserted in centers comes out clean. Cool in pans 15 minutes. Loosen loaves from pans. Invert onto cooling rack. Turn right sides up. Cool completely.

3. For caramel glaze, combine butter, brown sugar, granulated sugar and whipping cream in small heavy saucepan. Bring to a boil on medium heat; boil 1 minute. Remove from heat; cool 20 minutes. Add confectioners' sugar and vanilla extract; blend with wooden spoon until smooth and thick. Spread evenly on cooled loaves. Garnish with pecan halves and maraschino cherry halves before glaze sets.   *Makes 2 loaves (24 slices)*

Wolfman Cake

1 package (18¼ ounces) cake mix, any flavor, plus ingredients to prepare mix
1 container (16 ounces) chocolate frosting
1 container (16 ounces) caramel frosting
   Hard candies, nuts, large candy corn, yellow gummy worms and black jelly beans for decoration
   Black and red decorating gels

1. Preheat oven to 350°F. Prepare and bake cake mix according to package directions for 13×9-inch baking pan. Cool in pan on wire rack 15 minutes. Remove cake from pan; cool completely on wire rack.

2. Cut cake in half crosswise to form two 6½×4½-inch layers. Place 1 layer on serving platter. Spread ½ of chocolate frosting over bottom layer. Top with second layer. Spread remaining chocolate frosting over top and sides of cake.

3. Spoon caramel frosting over chocolate frosting. Use back of spoon to pull frosting into points to resemble fur. Decorate face with assorted candies and decorating gels as desired.   *Makes 12 servings*

The publisher would like to thank the companies and organizations listed below for the use of their recipes and photographs in this publication.

Cherry Marketing Institute

Crisco is a registered trademark of The J.M. Smucker Company

Duncan Hines® and Moist Deluxe® are registered trademarks of Pinnacle Foods Corp.

EAGLE BRAND®

Grandma's® is a registered trademark of Mott's, LLP

The Hershey Company

© Mars, Incorporated 2006

Nestlé USA

The Quaker® Oatmeal Kitchens

Watkins Incorporated

VOLUME MEASUREMENTS (dry)

$1/8$ teaspoon = 0.5 mL
$1/4$ teaspoon = 1 mL
$1/2$ teaspoon = 2 mL
$3/4$ teaspoon = 4 mL
1 teaspoon = 5 mL
1 tablespoon = 15 mL
2 tablespoons = 30 mL
$1/4$ cup = 60 mL
$1/3$ cup = 75 mL
$1/2$ cup = 125 mL
$2/3$ cup = 150 mL
$3/4$ cup = 175 mL
1 cup = 250 mL
2 cups = 1 pint = 500 mL
3 cups = 750 mL
4 cups = 1 quart = 1 L

VOLUME MEASUREMENTS (fluid)

1 fluid ounce (2 tablespoons) = 30 mL
4 fluid ounces ($1/2$ cup) = 125 mL
8 fluid ounces (1 cup) = 250 mL
12 fluid ounces ($1 1/2$ cups) = 375 mL
16 fluid ounces (2 cups) = 500 mL

WEIGHTS (mass)

$1/2$ ounce = 15 g
1 ounce = 30 g
3 ounces = 90 g
4 ounces = 120 g
8 ounces = 225 g
10 ounces = 285 g
12 ounces = 360 g
16 ounces = 1 pound = 450 g

DIMENSIONS

$1/16$ inch = 2 mm
$1/8$ inch = 3 mm
$1/4$ inch = 6 mm
$1/2$ inch = 1.5 cm
$3/4$ inch = 2 cm
1 inch = 2.5 cm

OVEN TEMPERATURES

250°F = 120°C
275°F = 140°C
300°F = 150°C
325°F = 160°C
350°F = 180°C
375°F = 190°C
400°F = 200°C
425°F = 220°C
450°F = 230°C

BAKING PAN SIZES

Utensil	Size in Inches/Quarts	Metric Volume	Size in Centimeters
Baking or Cake Pan (square or rectangular)	8×8×2	2 L	20×20×5
	9×9×2	2.5 L	23×23×5
	12×8×2	3 L	30×20×5
	13×9×2	3.5 L	33×23×5
Loaf Pan	8×4×3	1.5 L	20×10×7
	9×5×3	2 L	23×13×7
Round Layer Cake Pan	8×1½	1.2 L	20×4
	9×1½	1.5 L	23×4
Pie Plate	8×1¼	750 mL	20×3
	9×1¼	1 L	23×3
Baking Dish or Casserole	1 quart	1 L	—
	1½ quart	1.5 L	—
	2 quart	2 L	—